Otto von Bismarck **Empire's First**

About Charles River Editors

Charles River Editors provides superior editing and original writing services across the digital publishing industry, with the expertise to create digital content for publishers across a vast range of subject matter. In addition to providing original digital content for third party publishers, we also republish civilization's greatest literary works, bringing them to new generations of readers via ebooks.

Sign up here to receive updates about free books as we publish them, and visit Our Kindle Author Page to browse today's free promotions and our most recently published Kindle titles.

Introduction

Otto Von Bismarck

In 1832, 17 year old Otto von Bismarck had just entered university and was already rejecting the republican indoctrination of his grade school years. Unlike so many of his day who had championed representative government, Bismarck longed for the glory of a nation he believed would only be found under a single, strong leader. Though his early university days showed him he would be isolated by this thinking, he strongly believed not only in the ideal of a national German state, but in its possibility. In his memoirs, Bismarck recalls that at this young age, he "retained [his] own private National sentiments, and [his] belief that in the near future events would lead to German unity; in fact, [he] made a bet with [his] American friend Coffin that this aim would be attained in twenty years."[1]

Though it would take longer than he had predicted, Germany would eventually be united and he would be the person responsible for accomplishing it. Bismarck would go on to accomplish his goal and strengthen Germany into a modern political state by embracing specific political principles, despite their lack of popularity. Bismarck biographer Jonathan Steinberg refers to these principles as the "Prussian legacy," including "the army inherited from the 'genius King' Frederick the Great; the fusion of the Junker class with the army and the bureaucracy, the pervasive idea of '*Deinst*' or service; the rigid distinction between the nobility and the

[1] Bismarck, The Man and the Statesman; Being the Reflections and Reminiscences Of Otto, Prince Von Bismarck. Vol 1. Ed., A.J. Butler. New York, London, Harper & Bros. 1898, 2.

bourgeoisie; [and] a military conception of honor."

As "the most interesting character of the nineteenth century," Bismarck would spend his life in service of the Hohenzollern Kings, elevating William I from a Prussian King near abdication King to the first German emperor. He would alienate many along the way, but under William, he would retain what he wanted most: the power to shape Germany's future.

Otto von Bismarck: The Life and Legacy of the German Empire's First Chancellor looks at the life and work of Germany's most famous politician. Along with pictures of important people, places, and events, you will learn about Otto von Bismarck like never before.

Birth and Education

Otto von Bismarck was born to Ferdinand von Bismarck-Schönhausen and his wife, Wilhelmine Mencken, in 1815 in Schoenhausen, Prussia.[2] Otto Pflanze says, "His heritage was both bourgeois and aristocratic," the son of fifth generation nobility on his father's side and the civil service on his mother's. [3]

Bismarck's father was known as kind and well-intentioned, but he was considered the least talented of his brothers and more interested in social matters and entertainment than business or farming, his destined occupation. Though Bismarck did not struggle with loving his father, he did struggle with respecting him, as evidenced in a letter written to his fiancée years after his father's death[4]: "I really loved my father. When not with him I felt remorse concerning my conduct toward him and made resolutions that I was unable to keep for the most part. How often did I repay his truly boundless, unselfish, good-natured tenderness for me with coldness and bad grace? Even more frequently I made a pretense of loving him, not wanting to violate my own code of propriety, when inwardly I felt hard and unloving because of his apparent weakness. I was not in a position to pass judgment on those apparent weaknesses, which annoyed me only when coupled with gaucherie. And yet I cannot deny that I really loved him in my heart. I wanted to show you how much it oppresses me when I think about it."[5]

The Junker nobility to which Bismarck belonged was a service nobility with allegiance to the Prussian King. Unlike their noble counterparts in nearby nations, Prussian nobles knew little of individual power or extreme riches. Instead, "the Junkers were nearer to the soil, often milking their own cows and selling their wool themselves at the nearest market, sometimes distinguished from the more prosperous peasant-farmers only by their historic names."[6]

Bismarck's father led a relatively simple life and harbored no delusions about a change in family status. His management of the family estate proved so ineffectual he was forced to give up Schoenhausen and move to Kniephof, a smaller estate, soon after Bismarck was born.[7]

His mother, on the other hand, was far stricter with her son and ensured her children would be more highly educated than was typical of the rural Junker nobility.[8] Bismarck attended the Plamann Boarding School from the age of 6. Here and later at the Gymnasium in Berlin, he would receive a strong classical education.[9] He neither excelled at nor appreciated his education

---

[2] Kenneth Barkin, "Otto Von Bismarck", *The Latin Library*. <latinlibrary.com> Accessed October 7, 2017.

[3] Otto Pflanze, *Bismarck and the Development of Germany: The Period of Unification, 1815-1871* (Princeton, NJ: Princeton University Press, 1971), 49.

[4] Jonathan Steinberg. *Bismarck: A Life. Oxford: Oxford University Press*, 2011, 28-29.

[5]Ibid, 29.

[6] A. J. P. Taylor, Bismarck: The Man and the Statesman (New York: Knopf, 1955), 9.

[7] Ibid., 13.

[8] Otto Pflanze, 49.

[9] Ibid.

and resented his mother, even claiming to have "hated her." Wilhelmine Mencken had exposure to the royal court through her philosopher father until the age of 12. After his early death, Wilhelmine was reduced in her social status and married the 35-year-old Ferdinand at the age of 17. Steinberg theorizes that Wilhelmine suffered not only from an unhappy marriage, but disappointment in her attempts to live vicariously through her sons, who lacked her intellect or drive (at least as far as education was concerned). Her letter to Bismarck's older brother reveals the ire with which her children were met when they disappointed her: "I imagined that my greatest good fortune would be to have a grown son, who, educated under my very eyes, would agree with me, but as a man would called to penetrate deeper into the world of intellect than I as a woman could do. I rejoiced in the thought of the intellectual exchange, the mutual exchange for mental and spiritual engagement, and of that satisfying feeling to have such pleasures with a person who would be through the bonds of nature dearest to my heart, and who, still more, through the kinship of spirit, would draw ever closer to me. The time for these hopes to be fulfilled has arrived but they have disappeared and unfortunately, I must confess, forever."[10]

Bismarck's memories of the Plamann School were negative. The teachers, he had claimed, were "demagogic" and abusive, both waking and disciplining the children with "rapier blows."[11] Later, Bismarck's education at the Gymnasium further embittered him against his mother, since he preferred the farming life the country afforded. There, he learned English and French, German literature and music, as well as math and science. He appreciated many things he learned, but if Pflanze is correct, his education "provided him with quotations which later adorned his speech and writing but did not change his way of looking at life."[12]

Attending university in Hanover, Bismarck first proclaimed himself a liberal but grew more nationalistic over his years of exposure to "ill-bred students from the middle class,"[13] whom he despised. He spent more time making friends (two of which he would maintain for life) and drinking than studying and came home after just one year. One of his many biographers describes a young college student who was interested in creating an image "striding around Gottingen in unconventional clothes and accompanied by a large mastiff dog."[14] Bismarck had accrued debt in just a few months. As he stated in a letter to a friend, his "credit" continued to allow him to "live in a slovenly way."[15] His lifestyle, he said, had caused him to look ill, which he was sure "the old man, [would], of course ascribe when [he went] home for Christmas, to a lack of means of subsistence; then [he would] make a scene and say to him [he] would rather be a mohammedan than suffer hunger any longer, and that [would] solve the problem."[16] The contempt he had for his father, at least when out of his presence, is revealed here in ugly fashion.

---

[10] Jonathan Steinberg, 33.
[11] Ibid.
[12] Otto Pflanze, 50.
[13] A.J.P. Taylor, 14.
[14] Katherine Lerman, Bismarck: Profiles in Power. (London: Routledge; Taylor and Francis Group), 2004, 1.
[15] Steinberg, 42.
[16] Ibid.

At the University of Berlin, his academics improved slightly when he studied law, but he spent most of his time on history and German and English literature.[17]

Faith and Marriage

Following university, Bismarck tried his hand at a civil service job, had multiple high-profile affairs with English women in which he was largely humiliated, joined the army for an uninspiring year of service, and after his father's death, co-managed Kniephof with his brother for eight miserable years. At only 19 years of age, Bismarck had once sarcastically predicted what it would look like for him to become a country squire. He wrote to a friend that in 10 years, he would be "a well-fed Landwehr officer with a moustache [sic], who curses and swears a justifiable hatred of Frenchmen and Jews until the earth trembles, and beats his dogs and servants in the most brutal fashion, even if he is tyrannized by his wife. I will wear leather trousers and allow myself to be ridiculed at the Wool Market in Stettin, and when anyone calls me Herr Baron I'll stroke my moustache [sic] in good humor and sell two dollars cheaper. On the King's birthday I'll get drunk and shout "Vivat!" and in general get excited a lot and my every third word will be "On my honor!" and "A superb horse!" In short, I shall be happy in my family's rural circle, *car tel est mon Plaisir* [for such is my pleasure]."[18] It is no wonder, then, that A.J.P. Taylor describes Bismarck as "bitter, cynical and neurotic, his gifts running to nothing"[19] after less than a decade on the estate.

Somewhat suddenly, however, he sought to understand the faith of his Lutheran neighbors whom he believed to exhibit peace and contentment. For a man who had earned the nickname "The Mad Junker" for his wild ways during the years spent at Kniephof, Christianity offered him something different. In North Prussia, Schoenhausen was surrounded by Protestantism. Since Bismarck had left home at the age of 6 to be educated in the city and then later at university, he missed much of the religious education that would have taken place in the life of an ordinary Junker child. Instead, he was exposed to still-popular ideas of Enlightenment at Gottingen and left university a "pantheist," according to Taylor.[20]

At 16, Bismarck declared his lack of belief in God, reporting he had stopped saying his prayers. At that stage, Bismarck has been described variously as an atheist, a pantheist, and a deist. He explained his reason for abandoning prayer as being "because [it] seemed inconsistent with my view of God's nature; saying to myself, either God himself, being omnipresent, is the cause of everything even of every thought and volition of mine and so in a sense offers prayers to himself through me, or, if my will is independent of God's will, it implies arrogance and a doubt as to the inflexibility as well as the perfection of the divine determination to believe that it can be

---

[17] A.J.P. Taylor, 15

[18] Gordon A. Craig, *Theodor Fontane: Literature and History in the Bismarck Reich* (New York: Oxford University Press, 1999), 100.

[19] A.J.P. Taylor, 20.

[20] Ibid.,14.

influenced by human appeals."[21]

Bismarck at 21

At 32, he experienced conversion to Christianity under the guidance of friends Maria von Thadden and Moritz von Blanckenburg.[22] In gaining his faith, Bismarck also took a wife of Lutheran persuasion and a close companion of his religious mentor, Johanna von Puttkamer. He would write to her of his relationship with God only a few years later: "I am God's soldier, and must go wither He sends me, and I believe that He sends me and shapes my life as He requires."[23]

In marrying Johanna, Bismarck would have to convince his future father-in-law among others

[21] Charlton T. Lewis, ed., *The love letters of Bismarck; being letters to his fiancée and wife, 1846-1889*; authorized by Prince Herbert von Bismarck and translated from the German under the supervision of Charlton T. Lewis (New York: Harper, 1901), 4.

[22] George O. Kent, Bismarck and His Times (Carbondale, IL: Southern Illinois University Press, 1978), 7.

[23] George O. Kent, 7.

that he had meant to make a change in his lifestyle and attitudes. Here, he exhibited the life philosophy he had once expressed to a cousin: "I should like to make music as I want to, or I shall make none at all."[24] Opening his letter to Johanna's Pietist father with humble repentance, Bismarck made his case not on his own worthiness, but on his struggle to find and please God. After an invitation was extended by Johanna's father to visit the family, however, the humility in the letter seemed replaced with arrogance —Bismarck not only embraced Johanna when they met, to the astonishment of all concerned, but later at an informal dinner brazenly announced his intention of marrying her."[25]

Johanna

Bismarck's profession of faith has been seen as a turning point conversion by come and as a concession to his wife and her family by others. Taylor sees it as both, pointing to Bismarck's letter to his brother, whom Bismarck had formerly joined in skepticism, saying, "I think I am entitled to count myself among the adherents of the Christian religion. Though in many

[24] Ibid., 5.
[25] Ibid., 8.

doctrines, perhaps in those which they regard as essential, I am far removed from their standpoint, yet a sort of treaty of Passau has been silently established between us. Besides, I like piety in women and have a horror of feminine cleverness."[26] Other historians see Bismarck's conversion as genuine in the sense that all beliefs are, "because Bismarck himself recognized no standards except those that he applied himself…'It was not that Bismarck lied...but that he was finely attuned to the subtlest currents of any environment and produced measures precisely adjusted to the need to prevail. The key to Bismarck's success was that he was always sincere.'"[27] If this is so, we can believe that his religious conversion was the result of a spiritual struggle with doubt. As he described to his future father-in-law, "many an hour have I spent in disconsolate depression, thinking that my existence and that of others is purposeless and unprofitable perchance only a casual product of creation, coming and going like dust from rolling wheels."[28]

For those who take a critical view of Bismarck, his religion was simply an extension of his politics: "Bismarck's God was…fashioned for his own convenience, to provide comfort and security in his stormy existence as a dominant political figure."[29]

Through Bismarck's correspondence with Marie von Thadden, his religious mentor, it is apparent the two of them were in love, even though she married Moritz von Blankenberg, her intended. When his father and Marie died—the latter after only four months of marriage—Bismarck set upon a course of action, returning to his estate and marrying Johanna von Puttkamer to escape his loneliness.[30] Their marriage lasted 47 year. After asking for Johanna's hand in marriage and receiving her father's reluctant permission, Bismarck returned to Kniephof to put things in order with a new outlook: "The nearer I came to Schonhausen the more oppressive I found the thought of entering upon the old loneliness once more, for who knows how long. Pictures of a wasted past arose in me as though they would banish me from you…[yet] my whole view of life is a new one, and I am cheerful and interested even in my work on the dike and police matters. This change, this new life, I owe, next to God, to you, *ma tres chere, mon adoree Jeanneton* to you who do not heat me occasionally, like an alcohol flame, but work in my heart like warming fire."[31]

During their separation, Bismarck wrote Johanna regularly in letters that speak of a passionate love as well as almost fatherly instruction. During their engagement, Bismarck urged Johanna to polish her French so that she might not be "mortified" at a later time in which she might be called to use it socially. He also chided her regarding her vexation with a new horse and lovingly reproved her for her impatience for reunion: "In your actions, follow my words, not my works. Learn to take grateful pleasure, too, in the joy you have had, and do not cry, as little children do,

---

[26] A.J.P. Taylor, 20-21.
[27] George O. Kent, 9.
[28] Charlton T. Lewis, ed. 5.
[29] Edgar Feuchtwanger, "Bismarck, Prussia & German Nationalism," History Review, 2001.
[30] Jonathan Steinberg, 64.
[31] Ibid., 15.

'More!' the moment it stops."[32]

Bismarck's children circa 1855

Just before his marriage, Bismarck, an alternate delegate to the Prussian Parliament, was called upon to serve. "No one would ever have heard of me in my rural retreat, if I had not become a member of the united diet by chance," he later said.[33] This marked Bismarck's entry into politics. He wrote to Johanna because "[he] need[ed her] forgiveness very much," though the letter's purpose was also to explain that the offer had been impossible to turn down "without positively offending the Magdeburg estates and destroying every prospect [he had] which [was] based upon [his] relations with the estates."[34] This meant a prolonged delay in the reunion. Bismarck counseled his fiancée to "Be my strong Johanna, and thank God for all that has come to us, without complaint and sorrow about that which you might like to have different. We shall often

[32] Charlton T. Lewis, ed., 91.
[33] A.J.P. Taylor, 23.
[34] Charlton T. Lewis, 93.

be obliged to learn to set the cup down when it tastes the best; to rejoice in what we have drunk, and courageously to renounce what we must leave in it."[35]

Steinberg notes that Johanna would, even before her marriage, take second place to Bismarck's political ambitions, marKing his election to the Landtag as its start.[36] In his first appearance in the Landtag, Bismarck clearly sided with the conservatives against the liberals who were calling for a constitution.[37] Bismarck saw the Landtag's role as the body that approved taxation to serve the King's purposes.[38] His King, Friedrich William IV, found it necessary to call the German parliament to meet "because a combination of economic distress and intellectual discontent forced him to do so."[39] The Industrial Revolution was underway in Europe at the time, but Prussia lagged far behind, her economy looking more like Austria and Russia than Britain or the Netherlands.[40] Combined with frequent, poor harvests, heavy population growth, and unstable prices, this created a spirit of revolution in the least developed countries. Though Britain and the Netherlands would be spared, the rest of Europe would experience a series of failed but costly revolutions in the next year. In April of 1847, sensing the mood of the populous, the King warned, "There is no power on earth that can succeed in making me transform the natural relationship between prince and people…into a conventional constitutional relationship, and I will never allow a piece of written paper to come between the Lord God in heaven and this land."[41] Though members of the United Assembly were aghast at this pronouncement, their work continued, with about 70 ultra-conservatives, including Bismarck who joined with the King.[42]

Bismarck made his "maiden speech" on May 17th, 1847, which he described to an ailing Johanna in a letter the following day: "[Y]esterday raised an unheard-of storm of displeasure, in that, by a remark which was not explained clearly enough touching the character of the popular uprising of 1813, I wounded the mistaken vanity of many of my own party, and naturally had all the halloo of the opposition against me…I was reproached with my youth and all sorts of other things."[43] The speech raised the ire of the assembly chiefly due to Bismarck's apparent criticism of the Prussian "Revolution" of 1813. Bismarck seemed, to many of the assembly's liberals, to diminish the importance of the battles that had removed the French from Germany. Rather than a movement spawned from the desire of liberty over the tyranny of Emperor Napoleon, Bismarck claimed the battles that had expelled the French had been nothing more than the rightful duty of the Prussians, who, until that point, had been humiliated by a foreign power.

---

35 Ibid.
36 Jonathan Steinberg, 67.
37 George O. Kent, 9.
38 Steinberg, 73.
39 Ibid.
40 Ibid., 75.
41 Ibid., 76.
42 Ibid.
43 Charlton T. Lewis, 97.

To the liberals who had made up the majority of the assembly, the words had come as a shock. Bismarck appeared to have fully comprehended and enjoyed the response, pulling a newspaper from his pocket, turning his back, and reading silently while the Marshall attempted to quiet the assembly.[44] Steinberg remarks it contained all of the elements of his later speeches, including "complete contempt for the members of these bodies, dramatic gestures, [and] violent ideas couched in sparkling prose but delivered in easy conversational tones."[45]

With the assembly finished in late June, Bismarck completed business with his newfound political friends before heading to see Johanna.[46] During his months in the Landtag, there had been some discussion on the part of Johanna and her parents to suggest a delay of the wedding, perhaps even beyond that fall. Her illness, it was claimed, made putting off the wedding advisable, and if the wedding were to take place, there should be no honeymoon to save on expenses. To this, Bismarck responded with force, "The narrow-minded idea of taKing no journey this year, I have utterly dismissed from my mind. So far as expenses are concerned, it would cost exactly as much next year as this, and it makes practically not the least difference, if we have decided to travel, anyway, whether it takes place this year or later. But it is quite possible that next year you will not be quite so much in the humor and in a condition for travelling [sic] as you are in this, if I have the time and disposition for it, if we are both alive still, and if who knows what else? So, then, the upshot of it all is that we are to be married on the 24th, whether you are sick or well, and that, if the former is not the case to a greater degree than at present, we shall view the Alps from nearby. *Qu'en dis-tu*?"

Bismarck won the argument and the two were finally married July 28, 1847.[47]

---

[44] George O. Kent, 9.
[45] Steinberg, 77.
[46] George O. Kent, 1C.
[47] Ibid.

Bismarck in 1847

Political Advances

Conditions in Prussia and Europe, in general, were poor in 1848. Author of *Bismarck and His Times*, George O. Kent, lists the factors that made socialism attractive to the masses: poor wheat and rye crops, the potato blight, rising food prices and unemployment, and low wages.[48] An 1848 revolution ushered in a parliament elected through universal suffrage, but in the aftermath, as was the case with most conflicts in 1848, conservatism revived. Frederick William ended parliament and in its stead placed one with a more indirectly elected and less powerful membership. It was to this parliament, unlike the radical one, that Bismarck was elected.[49]

The Frankfurt Assembly began as a result of the 1848 revolution. Starting in 1851, Bismarck spent eight years as the Prussian envoy to the German Confederation in Frankfurt.[50] Before he

[48] Ibid., 14.
[49] A.J.P Taylor, 26.
[50] Edgar Feuchtwanger.

and Johanna headed to Frankfurt, Bismarck may have believed he needed to reassure Johanna of her role, as he wrote reassuringly, "I did not marry you in order to have a society wife for others but in order to love you in God and according to the requirements in my own heart, to have a place in this alien world that no barren wind can cool, a place warmed by my own fireplace, to which I can draw near while it storms and freezes outside. And I want to tend my own fire and lay on wood, blow the flames, and protect it and shelter it against all that is evil and foreign."[51]

During this time, there were several attempts at German unification. Both the ideas of "*Grossdeutschland* (Germany including Austria) and *Kleindeutschland* (Germany without Austria led by Prussia) had failed during the years of revolution."[52] While Bismarck's colleagues continued to fight the specter of socialist revolution which they believed was best countered with an alliance of conservative nations under the leadership of Metternich of Austria, Bismarck began to believe it was necessary to break, rather than reinforce, the traditional ties between confederation and Austrian dominance.[53] Though he may have arrived "with the sincere intention of co-operating with Austria,"[54] in the attitudes he adopted while serving in Frankfurt, Bismarck rejected, at least temporarily, two long-held conservative positions: the belief in the divine right of absolute monarchs and the necessity for the holy alliance between Germany, Austria, and Russia.[55]

When possible, Bismarck went out of his way to make friendships with the leaders of France, Russia, and England to put Austria on notice of Prussia's increasing status. Bismarck even suggested forming an alliance with Russia and France against the Austrians, though the idea was rejected by his own government.[56]

In Frankfurt, Bismarck's behavior was designed to indicate to the Austrians that a new day had come. Diet tradition was to hold the Austrians as preeminent, but Bismarck broke this tradition by putting himself on equal footing with Austrian representatives, negotiating without his jacket, and by smoking cigars, a diplomatic tradition formerly reserved for Austrians.[57] One member of the Prussian delegation saw Bismarck as an upstart, comparing the Prussians to a lottery winner who had based his annual budget on a one-time win.[58] It was, in part, the atmosphere of Austrian superiority that further goaded Bismarck into forming relationships with Russia, England, and France.

With Austria facing involvement in the Crimean War, Bismarck made sure Prussia's promises extended to neutrality in the Balkans, rather than as an agreement to fight alongside Austrian

---

[51] Katherine Lerman, 19.
[52] Edgar Feuchtwanger.
[53] Ibid.
[54] A.J.P. Taylor, 33.
[55] Edgar Feuchtwanger.
[56] George O. Kent, 24.
[57] A.J.P. Taylor, 34.
[58] Ibid.

conflicts. At the same time, Bismarck successfully kept Austria out of the German trade union, the *Zollverein*, which he hoped would be led by Prussia alone.[59] Though not foreseeable at the time, Austria's exclusion would mean the "Germany of the *Zollverein*, which was later Bismarck's Reich, became an economic power of the first order as the coal mines of the Ruhr expanded; Austria remained…relatively backward in the end."[60] Bismarck's time in Frankfurt served "his aim…to divide Germany with Austria, not to unite it."[61]

In convincing King Friedrich William IV of his positions on Austria, Bismarck largely failed. Though the King talked with Bismarck regularly—Taylor notes the significance of rail that allowed Bismarck to travel "from Frankfurt to Berlin like the pendulum of a clock"[62]—he did not act on his advice. To further complicate matters, the King "fell hopelessly insane"[63] in 1858, and Bismarck was forced to deal with the King's regent brother who was far less interested in Bismarck's theories.

By 1859, Bismarck's desire to part ways with Austria had concerned the new Regent King of Prussia, Prince Wilhelm, enough to replace him in Frankfurt.[64] Thus, Bismarck was transferred to St. Petersburg after having served eight years as Prussia's representative at the Federal Diet.[65] Breaking with custom as he often did, Bismarck refused to follow the "formalities of farewell" in Frankfurt.[66] Though he resented the transfer away from the political center, he used the time to establish friendly relations with relatives and friends of the Czar. Even from his new post, Bismarck continued to argue that taking a strong stand against Austria and possibly even going to war against her was the key to Germany's unification. While the Austrians fought the Italians over land claims in the Austro-Sardinian War, Bismarck insisted Prussia refrain from fighting on Austria's side. Before the new King arrived at a decision about Prussia's role, the Austrians gave up the fight in July of 1859.[67] Bismarck believed the regent had lost the opportunity to further establish Prussia against Austrian interests. After a prolonged illness forced an absence, his fortunes with the new ruler not improving, Bismarck returned to Russia and in his "honorable exile,"[68] worked to establish strong relations with the Russians, a policy that would prove important in gaining a future ally as well as in keeping Russia out of later conflicts with the Prussians, such as in the Franco-Prussian War.[69] Taylor notes that despite his frustrations with his own state's policy at the time, "St. Petersburg was the only capital Bismarck left without hating."[70]

---

[59] George O. Kent, 24-6.
[60] A.J.P. Taylor, 37.
[61] Ibid., 35.
[62] Ibid., 36.
[63] Ibid., 42.
[64] George O. Kent, 28.
[65] Ibid.
[66] A.J.P. Taylor, 43.
[67] George O. Kent, 29-30.
[68] Ibid., 31.
[69] Ibid.

Wilhelm

The regent William was crowned King after the death of his brother in 1861, and Bismarck had opportunity to speak with William frankly about the path to a united Germany able to free the Prussians from German domination, but his ideas were rejected. Instead, the new King reinstated his commitment to the principles of "legitimacy" for traditional nations and authority, believing that his conservative stance was not only right, but the best chance for preserving peace in Europe. This meant that the official position of the King was to reject revolution as well as nationalist movements, such as the one in Italy, which some Germans had hoped would be the model for an eventual German nation.

Bismarck was transferred to Paris in 1862, which was, for him, an even less important and more temporary post.[71]

---

[70] A.J.P. Taylor, 44.
[71] George O. Kent., 32.

Bismarck's time in Paris was frustrating, but the move would serve to catapult him to a powerful position in Prussia. In Paris, the new King concluded, Bismarck could be called upon if needed. The King faced major opposition in parliament and relations grew worse. Throughout his time in St. Petersburg, Bismarck was called upon for advice on the matter, yet the King usually acted on his own terms. It was, in fact, the King's refusal to give Bismarck a free hand over the military that kept him from gaining the prime ministership.[72]

Wilhelm had many doubts about Bismarck, calling his advice to refuse to side with Austria in Crimea "that of a 'schoolboy."[73] He replaced the conservative cabinet that had served his brother with moderate conservatives, including a few who had supported the revolution of 1848, to which Bismarck strongly objected.[74] The King (and his more liberal wife) naively believed the appointment of these men would give him "a new moral tone, obedience to the constitution, [and] reforms of a moderate nature, but no fundamental changes and no sacrifice of royal authority."[75]

Even so, Paris had changed once Bismarck had returned from St. Petersburg. In a conversation with a one-time liberal rival, he said, "Prussia is completely isolated…There is but one ally for Prussia, if she knows how to win and handle them...the German people!" By way of response, Bismarck said, "I am the same Junker of ten years ago...but I would have no perception and no understanding, if I could not recognize clearly the realities of the situation."[76] When King Wilhelm continued to ignore his advice, counteracting his proposals to the French, Bismarck decided that perhaps the best action was no action and that he should let the King reap the rewards of his own policy-making. Bismarck spent his time visiting England and Brussels and making connections with various influencers, but he did not communicate with Berlin.[77]

The situation in Germany worsened. The new, more liberal parliament demanded a change to the required three-year service of all Prussians to the military. The fight over the issues seems trivial, since the previous law had required two years of service. The larger issue was whether the Prussian force would be a "more conservative, royalist army," loyal to the King and "a reliable tool against domestic disturbances," or if reforms would continue to create a citizen force answering to the people rather than to the King.[78] On this issue and on the budget which the liberals had refused to approve without the rights to army reform, the King refused to budge. The King planned to abdicate the throne when the German foreign minister begged Bismarck to return to speak to him. When he received no reply, Bernstorff sent another, "*Periculum in mora. Dépêchez-vous,*" Danger in delay. Hurry up.[79]

---

[72] A.J.P. Taylor, 48-9.
[73] Otto Pflanze, Bismarck and the Development of Germany: The Period of Unification, 1815-1871 (Princeton, NJ: Princeton University Press, 1971), 120.
[74] Ibid., 121.
[75] Ibid.
[76] Ibid., 130.
[77] A.J.P. Taylor, 49.
[78] George O. Kent, 37.

Bismarck returned to Berlin on September 20th, 1862.[80] On the verge of abdication, Wilhelm agreed to meet with Bismarck at his most desperate point, a time George Kent calls "as decisive for the future of the two men as it was for the fate of Prussia-Germany."[81] Bismarck struck a much-needed balance in dealing with the King: he refused to limit himself by agreeing to the King's formal demands but at the same time, he declared his undying loyalty to Wilhelm as monarch. Impressed by Bismarck's determination and passion, the King gave the idea of abdicating up, naming Bismarck both prime and foreign ministers instead.[82] The agreement was that Bismarck "would always submit to the King's orders in the last resort even if he disagreed with them" if the King was willing to entertain Bismarck's thoughts.[83]

Despite Bismarck's promise, several historians claim at that point he had already determined the time of absolute monarchs was over, believing that compromise with parliaments and a fundamental change in the relations between Prussia and Austria would be necessary to bring about a united Germany.[84]

Bismarck (left) in the 1860s

---

[79] Ibid., 51.
[80] George O. Kent, 33.
[81] Ibid., 34.
[82] Ibid., 35.
[83] A.J.P. Taylor, 52.
[84] Arnold Blumberg, ed., Great Leaders, Great Tyrants?: Contemporary Views of World Rulers Who Made History (Westport, CT: Greenwood Press, 1995), 14.

Chief Minister

Bismarck as Chief Minister

At 47, Bismarck was finally in a position to directly influence the King, shaping the land into a new and unified Germany and guiding her through wars and uncertain times over the next 27 years. His belief that parliaments were a necessary evil did not mean he looked forward to working with them or that he respected their right to exist. In fact, Bismarck's opening words on becoming chief minister would be his most famous, discounting the power of words and calling, instead. on his trust in *blut und eisen*.

On September 30th, only a week after returning to Berlin, he delivered the now famous "Blood and Iron" speech to the budget commission of parliament: There are members of the National Association [Nationalverein]—of this association that has achieved a reputation owing to the justness of its demands—highly esteemed members who have stated that all standing armies are superfluous. Yes, if only a public assembly had this view! Would not a government have to reject this?!—There was talk about the 'sobriety' of the Prussian people. Yes, the great independence of the individual makes it difficult in Prussia to govern with the constitution (or to consolidate the constitution?); in France things are different, there this individual independence is lacKing. A constitutional crisis would not be disgraceful, but honorable instead. –Furthermore, we are perhaps too 'well-educated' to support a constitution; we are too critical; the ability to assess government measures and records of the public assembly is too common; in the country, there are a lot of catiline characters who have a great interest in upheavals. This may sound paradoxical, but everything proves how hard constitutional life is in Prussia. – Furthermore, one is too sensitive about the government's mistakes; as if it were enough to say 'this and that [cabinet] minister made mistakes, as if one wasn't adversely affected oneself. Public opinion changes, the press is not public opinion; one knows how the press is written; members of parliament have a higher duty, to lead opinion, to stand above it. We are too hot-blooded, we have a preference for putting on armor that is too big for our small body; and now we're actually supposed to utilize it. Germany is not looKing to Prussia's liberalism, but to its power; Bavaria, Württemberg, Baden may indulge liberalism, and for that reason no one will assign them Prussia's role; Prussia has to coalesce and concentrate its power for the opportune moment, which has already been missed several times; Prussia's borders according to the Vienna Treaties are not favorable for a healthy, vital state; it is not by speeches and majority resolutions that the great questions of the time are decided—that was the big mistake of 1848 and 1849—but by iron and blood.[85]

Not only did Bismarck's speech disturb some members of parliament, it disturbed the King himself, who set off for Berlin to dismiss the new chief minister. When he arrived, Bismarck convinced the King that his words had only been meant to communicate the King's authority to parliament. He suggested that they tame the parliament together if necessary. Wilhelm responded dramatically, predicting their deaths and recalling the beheading of England's Charles I after a conflict with his own parliament. According to Bismarck, the King had been too much under the influence of his wife. Wilhelm cried, "I can perfectly well see where all this will end. Over there, in front of the Opera House, under my windows, they will cut off your head, and mine a little while afterwards [sic]."[86] Bismarck convinced him that even this end could be honorable, or at least, "better…than surrender." Bismarck recounted the words he had used to convince the monarch of the honor of his possible death: "I, fighting for my King's cause, and your Majesty sealing with your own blood your rights as King by the grace of God…Your Majesty is bound to fight, you cannot capitulate; you must, even at the risk of bodily danger, go forth to meet any attempt at coercion."[87] At this, in Taylor's account, "The soldier-King could not run away from a fight. He drew himself up, according to Bismarck's account, like an officer responding to the command of a superior."[88]

Bismarck was back in the King's good graces but still attempting to deal with a parliament that refused to approve the budget without additional powers. After almost a month of trying to get the parliament to re-open the debate on the budget and offering to let the army reform bill come before the chamber, Bismarck had made no progress. Having lost patience with the game, he informed the parliament that their refusal to approve a spending plan meant the King would have to spend without their approval, effectively dismissing the parliament on October 13, 1862.[89]

---

[85] Otto von Bismarck, Reden 1847-1869 [Speeches, 1847-1869], ed., Wilhelm Schüßler, vol. 10, Bismarck: Collected Works, ed. Hermann von Petersdorff. Berlin: Otto Stolberg, 1924-35, pp. 139-40.
[86] Paul Lay, "Interview: Jonathan Steinberg." History Today, Volume 2, Issue 9, September 2012.
[87] Ibid.
[88] A.J.P. Taylor, 57.
[89] Ibid, 58.

It is important to note the liberals in parliament considered Bismarck "an arch-conservative," while the conservatives called him "too liberal."[90] The King, though ostensibly ready to die with him, retained a basic distrust of Bismarck's decision-making, an attitude supported by Augusta, the King's wife and a life-long enemy of Bismarck. Their distrust was, perhaps, because at that point, Bismarck was neither loyal to the conservatives, the liberals, nor the King, but to his own beliefs that Germany must become a great nation. Bismarck knew what it would take for this to occur. He also knew that neither the current parliaments nor the King were ready to accept this reality in 1862. Visiting England's Disraeli during his time of self-imposed silence with the King, Bismarck predicted, "I shall soon be compelled to undertake the conduct of the Prussian government. My first care will be to reorganize the army, with or without the help of the Landtag [the legislature]...As soon as the army shall have been brought into such a condition to inspire respect, I shall seize the first best pretext to declare war against Austria, dissolve the German Diet, subdue the minor states, and give national unity to Germany under Prussian leadership."[91]

Though he was working for what he considered a weak King, Bismarck nevertheless had "a power base of one."[92] This meant that throughout the 26 years during which Bismarck served as the King's chief minister, he had to put up with the King's indecision and fear. He could never act freely, but would need to cajole, threaten, woo, or do whatever was necessary to accomplish his goals. At that time, Steinberg notes, Bismarck submitted eleven letters of resignation to the King, each of them rejected. This, too, was part of Bismarck's strategy.[93] Taylor explains that the controversy between King and parliament had to continue in order for Bismarck to stay in power. When, a year later, it appeared that parliament was interested in a true compromise with the King over army reform, Bismarck ensured it would never take place. After all, "the conflict…was the essential condition of his political existence."[94]

Bismarck's Wars

Ultimately, the most important conflicts for Bismarck's success would be military in nature.

A brief history of the complicated history of Denmark is necessary in order to understand Bismarck's actions in 1864. As Erich Eyck puts it, the Kingdom of Denmark, after the Congress of Vienna in 1815, included Denmark proper, and the duchies of Holstein, a German-dominated state to the south of the Jutland Peninsula, and Schleswig, a mixed duchy of both German and Danish loyalties. The death of the Danish King in 1863 brought a new and disputed Dane to the throne and re-opened the questions of loyalty and connection to the German Confederation in the duchies.[95] The now-deceased Frederick VII had attempted to incorporate Schleswig into

---

[90] George O. Kent, 40.
[91] Paul Lay, "Interview: Jonathan Steinberg." *History Today*, Volume 2, Issue 9, September 2012.
[92] Ibid.
[93] Ibid.
[94] A.J.P. Taylor, 59.
[95] Erich Eyck, Bismarck and the German Empire. (New York: W.W. Norton and Company, 1968), 77-8.

Denmark while leaving Holstein to remain part of the German Confederation in violation of the earlier treaty and the London protocol of 1852. According to the protocol—which had been endorsed by the major powers—Schleswig and Holstein would remain independent from Denmark, though closely tied to each other and the German-speaKing Holstein in the German Confederation. At Frederick's death, many Germans saw the chance to right the King's wrongs in his violating the protocol with the November Constitution, the document joining Schleswig with Denmark. Bismarck decided to play a wait-and-see game. His main concern was the port of Kiel, which he wanted for Prussia alone. Bismarck hoped the developing situation over the Schleswig-Holstein question would allow him to enter the situation militarily, as Prussia had in 1848. German nationalists, who believed the new King might attempt to incorporate Schleswig, Holstein, or both into Denmark, supported Duke Frederick of Austenburg as a replacement, hoping, instead, that Schleswig and Holstein would declare their independence from Denmark.[96]

Bismarck in 1863

In February of 1864, after the Danes had refused to revoke the November Constitution, troops

[96] George O. Kent, 48.

from both Prussia and Austria entered Schleswig to prevent its annexation. France, Russia, and Britain had already decided the defense of the Danes, who had violated their promises to the great powers, was not worth a war, though the angry British plenipotentiary had called Bismarck "a man without faith and law." Frankfurt liberals attempted to defy Bismarck and drive him from office with the refusal to support an invasion of Denmark. Instead, they found momentum with the Nationalist impulse and the great powers that were unwilling to decisively intervene on Denmark's behalf. By October, Denmark had ceded three of its former duchies—Schleswig, Holstein, and Lauenburg—to Prussia and Austria.[97]

Almost immediately following the victory, Prussia and Austria were in conflict regarding how the new territories would be ruled. Historians debate Bismarck's motives here; had he simply wanted to rule the new territories as a plan to strengthen Prussia itself or was his insistence at controlling Schleswig-Holstein part of a plan to draw Austria into a conflict, finally uniting German as a separate nation?[98] *The New York Times* reported on "The Schleswig-Holstein Question" in June of 1865, calling the escalating tension between Austria and Prussia "entertaining":

> "Each of these powers entered into the war against Denmark with the full intention of cheating each other, and pocketing the lion's share of the spoils…no sane man out of Germany ever believed that the crusade against the little mother kingdom was begun for the purpose of delivering the Schleswig-Holsteiners from Danish rule. Everybody knew that Prussia had an eye on Kiel, as a commodious harbor for her prospective navy. Austria wanted another ally among the small German States that support her against Prussia, and assist in checkmating the ambitious designs of king WILHELM and Herr BISMARCK…the people at large supported the war from a vague notion that it might lead to grand results in the way of German unity, that unfulfilled dream of many centuries.
>
> "…with the conclusion of peace came bitter jealousies, accusations and recriminations, that threaten to set all Germany together by the ears. Prussia, having the most to gain, made the first dash for the spoils. She seized upon the important seaport of Kiel, and commenced there the erection of fortifications and dockyards, with the aid of a person that felt entirely at home and meant to stay. When Austria remonstrated, Count BISMARCK serenely smiled, and uttered a few "glittering generalities" about the glory of Prussia being inseparably entwined with that of all the German States…Like a prudent statesman, he is content to move slowly, occasionally throwing a little dust in his adversary's eyes. He still keeps up a show of negotiation with Austria and the Federal Diet, and even proposes to allow the people of Schleswig-Holstein to express their sentiments

[97] Ibid., 50.
[98] Ibid.

through on election, which he well knows will do them no possible good, nor stand in the way of the accomplishment of his own designs."[99]

It is interesting to note the prominence of Bismarck in this article. Even to a foreign audience, it was clear Bismarck had controlled the strings in Prussia and that his ulterior motives ruled the day. By August, a treaty between Austria and Prussia had averted war. Prussia took Lauenburg and would administer the duchy of Schleswig and Austria of Holstein in the Treaty of Gastein.[100]

The question persists where Bismarck is concerned of whether he was a power-hungry manipulator who used war to his advantage, willing to embrace realpolitik whenever necessary, or whether he viewed war as the only means to accomplish the desires of his people to have a German national state. Taylor argues an alternate view, asserting that Bismarck disliked war as a means of settling disputes and only went to war when other means had failed: "[War] deprived him of control and left the decision to generals whose ability he distrusted. A civilian to the core, he always wanted to back a certain winner; and Moltke, the greatest Prussian general, told him repeatedly that nothing was certain in war."[101]

An 1867 political cartoon depicting all the roles and positions Bismarck seemed to have

[99] "Prussia and Austria: The Schleswig Holstein Question." *The New York Times*, June 11, 1865.
[100] A.J.P. Taylor, 78.
[101] Ibid., 80.

Nevertheless, Bismarck is repeatedly recorded in history as having "goad[ed] Austria into war" in 1866. Despite this, "it is impossible to point to the exact moment when Bismarck decided to go to war against Austria. As usual, he kept his options open and pursued several policies simultaneously."[102] Thus, Bismarck considered both Italy and France as potential allies in a future war with Austria. Both Italy and France believed they would gain territorially by allying themselves with the stronger Prussia, and Bismarck kept both ministers informed of his proceedings as a result. The Prussians accused Austria of mishandling Holstein's administration, of turning the Danes in Schleswig against Prussian rule, and of secretly supporting Duke Frederick of Austenburg as the rightful ruler of both. Public opinion, Bismarck believed, did not put enough stock in the importance of these matters to merit war with Austria.[103] Rather, he would need something more unifying to get Prussians on board.

Given a three-month military alliance with the Italians, time was of the essence. He proposed universal suffrage, hoping for a wave of enthusiasm from the German people, but was met with resistance from both the king and the people on his foreign policy instead. Bismarck needed to consider both the Italian and French reaction before any military move.[104] He increased pressure on the Austrians, threatening to arrest the Duke of Austenburg and arresting a member of the pro-Austrian press. By January of 1866, Bismarck informed Austrian Minister Benedetti "he considered the intimacy of the courts of Vienna and Berlin as over."[105] Because the German Confederation had ruled out an alliance between one of its states and a foreign power, the treaty with the Italians "was incompatible with the very existence of the Confederation,"[106]and kept secret.

Fearing war, Austria was forced to begin her mobilization. Unlike her more efficient Prussian neighbor, Austria would take six weeks to ready for war (some historians estimate as many as twelve).[107] Plagued by internal problems with Hungary, a limited budget, and limited public support for war, Austria began preparations desperate for a way out. To Bismarck's disappointment, an agreement was reached between Austrian and Prussian envoys: Austria would demobilize in exchange for Prussia doing the same. The peace was frustrated by the Italians, who had mobilized on Austria's western front. To demobilize at that point would be suicide, the Austrian government had claimed, much to Bismarck's delight; it now looked as if war was inevitable.

The Austrian government appealed to German member states at the Frankfurt Diet, calling for the mobilization of their armies to defend against Prussian aggression. A Bavarian member

---

102 George O. Kent, 52.
103 Ibid., 54-55.
104 Erich Eyck.
105 Ibid.
106 Ibid.,
107 Geoffrey Wawro, *The Austro-Prussian War: Austria's War with Prussia and Italy in 1866*. (New York: Cambridge University Press, 1997), 50.

offered an amendment which would exclude both Austria and Prussia from responding in a half-way measure designed to avoid war. Bismarck had his response prepared—no matter the outcome of the Frankfurt vote, Bismarck decided that any Austrian arrangement with a German state against Prussia was a violation of the German Confederation's constitution.[108]

The Austro-Prussian War began. In his answer to the question of Bismarck's true intentions regarding Austria, Erich Eyck has stated in a series of lectures given at Harvard that "although Bismarck was not from the beginning bent on war with Austria, he was engaged in a policy which made war unavoidable. The mistake of the Austrian statesmen was that they did not see in time that war was indeed inevitable, and that military and political preparations were necessary; but they cannot be reproached with having failed to avoid a war which was in no way avoidable."[109]

Bismarck and the German General Moltke were frustrated by King Wilhelm's limited response, not wanting to go to war with "brother Austria", while Bismarck argued that "it would be shrewder to bring about [a war] when the situation is favorable to us than to wait until Austria starts it in conditions advantageous to herself."[110]

For most historians, it was Prussia's military and economic superiority and not Bismarck's leadership that should be credited for the victory over the Austrians. Prussia's railroads and communication lines, its ability to lean on trained conscripts in reserve, and its superior weaponry in the breech-loading needle gun all led to a Prussian victory in only seven weeks of war.[111] By July 3rd, Sadawa had been won in a decisive battle.

Bismarck, it seems, is credited not only with military expertise, but with skillful navigation of international affairs at their most intense, but if he had always intended to fight the Austrians, he blazed a path to the goal that remains largely undetectable to today's analysts and historians. Instead, it was his desire to accomplish greater goals that made immediate decisions harder to predict. In fact, Bismarck was careful in his execution of the war against the Austrians, as well as ending it. As he recalled in his memoirs, "it would be of great importance whether the feelings we left behind in our opponents were implacable or the wounds we had inflicted on them and their self-respect were incurable. Moved by this consideration, I had a political motive for avoiding, rather than bringing about, a triumphal entry into Vienna in the Napoleonic style. In positions such as ours was then, it is a political maxim after a victory not to enquire how much you can squeeze out of your opponent, but only to consider what is politically necessary."[112] Bismarck believed a new Northern German Confederation was a political necessity. The

[108] Erich Eyck.
[109] Ibid..
[110] Geoffrey Wawro, 51.
[111] Robert Pearce, "The Austro-Prussian War: Robert Pearce Examines the Factors That Led to Prussia's Victory in the German Civil War of 1866," *History Review*, no. 66 (2010).
[112] Bismarck, The Man and the Statesman; Being the Reflections and Reminiscences of Otto, Prince Von Bismarck. Vol 2., Ed., A.J. Butler. New York, London, Harper & Bros. 1898, 43.

unification of the south and the formation of German as a nation state would have to wait.

In the immediate aftermath of the Austro-Prussian victory, Bismarck enjoyed political favor, if not a consolidated base of support, as the Prussian mood seemed to have swung in the direction of the pragmatic: "Prussia's victory of 1866 seemed to convince many of the advantages of the realpolitik of the 1860s over the idealism of the 1840s. People wearied of supporting the unsuccessful policies of Austria and were frustrated by the seemingly unattainable goals of liberalism and constitutionalism. But beyond that, the unification of the country under Prussian leadership now seemed within reach."[113]

From 1867, Bismarck played a waiting game where the unification of Germany was concerned, as the joining of the southern states—initially resistant to Prussian rule, friendly with Austria, and bent on independence—would have to be overcome. What was needed was "a clear case of French aggression"[114] toward either Prussia or the southern states. Not only would such a move by Napoleon III trigger the terms of the treaty between the German states, but it would keep the remaining world powers out of the conflict.[115]

---

[113] George O. Kent, 62.
[114] Ibid., 67.
[115] Ibid.

Napoleon III

It would be a dispute over the throne of Spain that would cause Napoleon III to act. During a revolution, Queen of Spain Isabella was forced to flee Madrid. Spain was divided over who would rule, and the other European nations had a decided interest in the matter. In the months that followed, Prince Leopold of Hohenzollern was suggested as a fitting heir. His name, as well as many others, circulated amongst the powerful and the influential. Some have suggested Bismarck had orchestrated the naming of Leopold as successor to tie Spain to Germany, but most historians dispute his direct involvement in the matter. Leopold's attractions included the fact that he was "the husband of a Portuguese princess, related both to the royal house of Prussia and to Napoleon III, and with several sons to carry on the line."[116] Though many candidates were considered—including Leopold's younger brother, Charles, who was a ruling Romanian prince—they were deemed unacceptable to some party of influence in heavily fractious Spain, unacceptable to hold such a great power, or they were uninterested.

Bismarck believed Leopold's acceptance of the crown would be an advantage for Prussia,

---

[116] Lawrence D. Steefel, Bismarck, the Hohenzollern Candidacy, and the Origins of the Franco-German War of 1870 (Cambridge, MA: Harvard University Press, 1962), 22.

though Napoleon had announced his opposition to Leopold. Bismarck wrote to convince his king, "In the long run, we must expect the preservation of peace, not from the goodwill of France, but from her impression of the strength of our position."[117]

The reaction to Spain's surprise announcement regarding Leopold provoked outrage across France, given the general feeling that his candidacy had been a plot hatched by Bismarck and that France would simply never accept a Hohenzollern on the Spanish throne. After much internal debate in the houses of Prussia, Leopold's name was withdrawn, but for an angry Napoleon III, this was not enough. He demanded Wilhelm provide "a written guarantee of Leopold's refusal and a promise not to revive the candidacy in the future."[118]

Bismarck did not care much for control of the Spanish throne, but for world perception with respect to French influence in Prussian affairs. For William to have given in to this pressure, for Leopold to have withdrawn and France to feel as if she had "won," was unacceptable. Reading the king's conciliatory telegrams to the French enraged Bismarck, who considered resigning.[119] When Bismarck received the king's account of his interview with the French ambassador, he edited the language to make the confrontation between William and French Ambassador Benedetti more combative than it had been in an attempt to recover Prussian dignity. Bismarck's account read, "After the news of the renunciation of the Prince von Hohenzollern had been communicated to the Imperial French government by the Royal Spanish government, the French Ambassador in Ems made a further demand on His Majesty the king that he should authorize him to telegraph to Paris that His Majesty the king undertook for all time never again to give his assent should the Hohenzollerns once more take up their candidature. His Majesty the king thereupon refused to receive the Ambassador again and had the latter informed by the adjutant of the day that His Majesty had no further communication to make to the Ambassador."[120]

The impertinence of the French toward the Prussian king, the Hohenzollerns, and their presumption of right in the matter quickly turned public opinion against the French in Prussia and Germany. Bismarck fanned the flames by taking an offended tone. "It was impossible that Prussia could tamely and quietly sit under the affront offered to the king and to the nation by the menacing language of the French government," he said.

Believing France had prepared for success in a quick war against the Prussians, Napoleon took the bait and declared war against Prussia on July 19, 1870.[121] The French declared war as much against Bismarck as they had against Prussia, believing he had manipulated the Spanish ascendancy in an effort to seek power, rather than peace. A wartime poem reveals this animosity for Bismarck rather than his German "slaves," as felt in France at the outset of war:

---

[117] Ibid., 58.
[118] George O. Kent, 70.
[119] Lawrence D. Steefel, 166.
[120] Ems Telegram, 1870. World War One Primary Documents. <www.firstworldwar.com>
[121] George O. Kent, 71.

“Who is this G[erman] fat but quick?
The hound that crouched ’neath B[ismarck’]’s stick
What time the plunderers of the Dane
Quarrelled about their shameless gain.
Beery and fat and scant of wind
He puffs along the battle plain
For is not B[ismarck]’s ‘stick’ behind?
Who’s dead to honor, lives to pain.
This is your G[erman], fat yet quick
Driven to war by B[ismarck]’s stick.
What is this G[erman]’s lawful prize?
Whate’er finds favor in his eyes.
The accursed one who hounds him on
Knows well his self-respect is gone.
He fears his reckless discontent,
And so in devilish mood
Delighted sees it find a vent
In rapine lust and blood.
That is this German’s lawful prize
Whate’er finds favor in his eyes.
What does his master hope to gain?
That does not seem so very plain.
To inscribe in each historic tome
Another rush of Goths to Rome?
Seeks he the immortality
Of him who fired Diana’s shrine,
Or with the ambition cursed is he
With Caliph Omar’s fame to shine?
What then does B[ismarck] hope to gain?
I give it up—my quest is vain—
But what then will this G[erman] gain?
The answer is both full & plain—
Contempt from every honest man
The thief’s reward, the murderer’s ban,
When Europe’s slow but sure police
Are set upon his bloody track
And all shall feel that lasting peace
Requires he should be beaten back.
These will the rabid Germain gain
Fettered at length in Europe’s chain.

But are not G[erman]s civilized?
Is justice not among them prized?
These statements which have long been made
But yesterday were not gainsaid
But he who runneth now may read
Unlikely as it may seem
This quiet content, devoid of greed
Is but an empty dream.
For Germans are not civilised
Say rather they are brutalized.
What should the wretched F[rench]man feel,
Downtrodden by the G[erman]'s heel?
Glad that the veil is drawn aside
Which did so long the monster hide
That lust of Blood & Rapine rife
Are plainly now revealed
Which secretly preparing strife
Were but by Tartuffe's cant concealed.
This satisfaction he may feel
Though crushed beneath that brutal heel…
But, Frenchman, though thou feel the curse,
Rejoice—thy foeman's case is worse.
When from his hordes thy land is free
Thou shalt enjoy thy liberty—
He, crushed beneath an iron hand,
With none from 'stick' to save,
May yell in praise of Vaterland
But is not less a Slave!
Hurrah—each mangy skulking hound
In Bismark's leash is firmly bound.
All honor, Bismark, to thy stick
Which makes thy beery slaves so quick—
But act with caution—have a care—
And dread the vigor of despair!
Even Germans may at last feel shame
The 'stick' so long to bear
Syne play to thee this pleasant fame
For 'turn about' is fair.
And Frenchman will pronounce it 'chic'
When Bismark's slaves give him the 'stick.'"[122]

Unfortunately for the author, French hopes of victory were destroyed by September when the French were soundly defeated at the battle of Sedan and Napoleon was captured.[123] Refusing to admit defeat, the citizens of Paris formed a wartime republic, and the Prussian army began a month-long siege of the city that would not end until February 1871. The Parisian hope for Austrian, British, or Russian support was crushed, and the Prussians ended the bitter conflict with new territory in Alsace-Lorraine, a promise of five billion francs to be paid, and the right for German forces to occupy a portion of northern France.[124] Wilhelm I was crowned Emperor of Imperial Germany at Versailles, a humiliation the French would not soon forget.

A painting depicting the surrender of Napoleon III

[122] P.G. Tait's poem on Bismark [sic.] ELIZABETH F. LEWIS (NEE RUDGE) University of St. Andrews April 22, 2012

[123] George O. Kent, 72.

[124] Ibid., 72-4.

A painting depicting Wilhelm I's coronation as emperor

The biggest win for Prussia was her emergence as Germany, a new and united power. As one German had put it, "Now that we have achieved the most cherished dream of our lives, what is there left to live for?"[125] The answer would prove elusive to Bismarck, who, with 25 years left in power, seemed to enjoy little of the spoils of German public life. He despised court life, preferring to live on his old and new lands at Varzin and Friedrichsruh, his gift from King Wilhelm.[126] As one biographer asserts, "The one thing which really laid Bismarck low was boredom. He could always rise to an emergency and work with a penetration and efficiency that few men have shown. But he needed to live in a crisis all the time."[127]

Kulturkampf

One relief for Bismarck was his engagement with the Catholic Church over southern Germany. Determined not to let his great work of unification fail, Bismarck set out to counter what he saw as the corrupting influence of Catholicism in the south.

In the mid-1860s, Pope Pius IX declared that men erred if they proceeded on the assumption that "the Pope can and must compromise and be reconciled with progress, liberalism, and modern culture."[128] The pope represented conservatism and opposed the new, modern German

---

[125] Ibid, 77.
[126] A.J.P. Taylor, 134.
[127] Ibid., 137-8.

state that was being built at the expense of traditional Catholic powers in Italy, France, and Austria. This established a natural enmity between Bismarck and the Church. In the face of the pope's claim of infallibility, Bismarck launched a campaign to diminish the influence of the Catholic Church and the political opposition he was sure accompanied it.

Pope Pius IX

[128] Ibid., 148.

Bismarck, as was the case in the Hohenzollern candidacy, put much weight on appearances. He simply could not stand the thought of the king, the nation, or himself bowing to pressure from a foreign power, including that of the pope. Recalling the humiliation of an earlier German king at the hands of religious authorities, he emphatically stated, "Depend upon it, in nominating a cardinal as our representative at Rome, we neither hoped to talk the pope over to our way of thinking, nor did we at all wish to signify our willingness to repeat a certain ceremony enacted centuries ago at Canossa."[129] Bismarck—and Wilhelm by extension—would never beg for mercy outside the Vatican. His words on the relations between German leadership and the now infallible head of the Church seemed designed to distance the relationship: "We were neither confident enough to expect that [we would] succeed in shaking those strong convictions which have induced his holiness to adopt his recent attitude toward us and the world at large; nor could we, after the new dogmas promulgated by him, think of concluding a concordat with the possessor of supernatural wisdom and power. In point of fact, I am sorry to say, after the prerogative lately assumed by the pope, that no government which is not prepared to see the secular power annihilated and placed under spiritual jurisdiction, will consent to conclude a concordat."[130]

When he demanded more respect for the German representative to the Vatican, Bismarck was met with resistance from the pope, who insisted on his sovereignty. He replied with a lesson from history, sarcastically stating, "As for his defining the relations between pope and cardinal as those between master and servant, I beg to ask one so deeply versed in ecclesiastical history whether Cardinals Mazarin and Richelieu, when prime ministers of France, were the employees of the pope or the advisors and ministers of their respective sovereigns."[131]

Bismarck's response to the Catholic Church was not limited to words. As soon as the war against France had concluded, he abolished the Catholic Bureau of Worship and put public religious matters under Protestant control.[132] Over the next year, he promoted the passing of laws forbidding Catholics from criticizing the government, effectively outlawed Catholic education, and cut off the Jesuits and Germany's official relations with the Vatican.[133]

Though the religious laws were not directed exclusively at the Catholic Church, it represented the main opposition that was Bismarck's concern. If the Protestant Church had helped a source of opposing power, he would certainly have targeted it more directly. The Kulturkampf had reached its height with the enforcement of the May Laws of 1873, which were said by Germany's minister of worship, Albert Falk, "to secure the indispensable rights of the state while rejecting interference in purely ecclesiastical affairs."[134] These laws were so restrictive that most

---

129 Francis W. Halsey and William Jennings Bryan, eds., *The World's Famous Orations, vol. 7* (New York: Funk and Wagnalls, 1906), 244.
130 Ibid., 245.
131 Ibid., 247.
132 Michael Cook, "How Bismarck Lost Kulturkampf.", *Crisis Magazine*, July 17, 2012.
133 Ibid.

of Germany's Catholic clergy left the country or were arrested within three years.[135]

An 1875 political cartoon depicting Bismarck confronting the pope

By 1878, a new pope and socialist pressures in Germany made Bismarck see German Catholics in a more positive light. As always, his political concerns trumped his philosophical ones, and Bismarck sought to deal with the socialist threat.[136] The Kulturkampf was over.

---

134 Robert W. Lougee. "The Kulturkampf and Historical Positivism." Church History 23, no. 3 (1954): 219.
135 George O. Kent, 85.
136 Michael Cook.

Political Changes in Germany

Bismarck in 1875

Though he opposed socialism as an idea, since the 1862 constitutional crisis that had brought him to office, Bismarck had entertained the idea of socialism as a means of consolidating power. He had learned from the socialists that votes could be bought with "material rewards…that universal suffrage is counter-revolution."[137]

For years, Bismarck relied on a split between the two major German Socialist parties to prevent their gaining ground. In 1875, however, the parties combined to form the Social Democratic Labor Party of Germany (SPD).[138] Though Bismarck feared the Socialists, he was still busy with the Kulturkampf in 1875 and had alienated the center party with his anti-Catholic stance. Three years later, the Socialists seemed to merit more serious consideration. Having gained seats in the Reichstag and having made two separate assassination attempts on the king,

[137] A.J.P. Taylor, 60.
[138] George O. Kent, 89.

Bismarck decided that the time to deal with them had come. Unable to outlaw the party directly, he dismissed the 1878 Reichstag with the hope of destroying the power of both the opposition Liberals and Socialists at once.

Then, "convinced of the righteousness of his cause and the reasonableness of his policy, Bismarck attempted to deal with the workers in two ways: repressive measures to destroy the workers' organizations and turn them away from the anti-religious, materialistic teachings of Marx and Engels, and governmental social measures which would, at the same time, bind them to the state."[139] This meant that while Bismarck would repress the SPD with laws restricting their rights to assemble and to publish, he would mitigate the people's response by agreeing to specific and popular social legislation to gain the support of Germany's growing working classes, whose numbers had increased during the Industrial Revolution. These workers were also voters, who identified with the Socialist Party and were looking for economic benefits, rather than societal revolution.

In meeting these needs, Bismarck said, "My idea was to bribe the working classes, or shall I say, to win them over, to regard the state as a social institution existing for their sake and interested in their welfare."[140] An old-age pension would be the crowning achievement of Bismarck's socialist-style reforms, provided out of his desire for control, as he had observed that "whoever has a pension for his old age is far more content and far easier to handle than one who has no such prospect."[141] He also pushed for social welfare legislation, including accident insurance and disability insurance by 1889.[142] Here, as in other domestic battles, Bismarck was more frustrated than successful. Though he avoided a full-scale Socialist revolution in Germany, he was unable to defeat the socialist party in the Reichstag, which continued to make gains.

Bismarck continued his foreign policy efforts by attempting to ensure Germany's security and supremacy. While he rejected the idea of colonization at first, thinking it expensive, resource-consuming, and potentially problematic for relations with other nations, he soon became convinced that Germany should move forward with a colonial empire. His support, he claimed, was not due to a change of mind about colonization in general, but an allowance for "the responsibility for the material development of a colony, as well as its inauguration, to the action and the enterprise of our seafaring and trading citizens…to proceed less on the system of annexing the transoceanic provinces to the German Empire than that of granting charters, after the form of the English Royal Charters."[143]

---

[139] Ibid., 94.

[140] Richard M. Ebeling. "Marching to Bismarck's Drummer: The Origins of the Modern Welfare State." *Foundation for Economic Education*. December 1, 2007.

[141] A.J.P. Taylor, 203.

[142] Lorraine Boissoneault. "Bismarck Tried to End Socialism's Grip—By Offering Government Healthcare." *Smithsonian Magazine*. July 14, 2017.

[143] Bismarck on "Pragmatic" Colonization (June 26, 1884) Forging an Empire: Bismarckian Germany (1866-1890) German History in Documents and Images.

Thus, on the morning of Saturday, November 15, 1884, plenipotentiaries of all of the major powers of Europe gathered at Bismarck's official residence. As each entered the yard, they were met at their carriage door by Bismarck himself and then ushered into the library, where an informal reception took place. Then, as a body, they climbed the wide, ceremonial staircase to a second-floor reception room, where each took his allocated seat at a semi-circular table arranged before a large and detailed map of Africa pinned to the wall. Bismarck addressed the assembled delegates, outlining briefly the objectives of the meeting, after which, casting his eyes from left to right, he declared the Berlin Conference formally in session.

A depiction of Bismarck at the Berlin Conference

The Berlin Conference of 1884-1885, a dry and rather formal affair, was nonetheless one of the most important and far-reaching gatherings of international powers to take place at any time during the 19th century, and one that would deeply impact the course of European and African history up to the present day. In its simplest terms, the Berlin Conference sought to regulate the subdivision of Africa between the principal European powers in a manner that would not cause a major war between them.

Only a somewhat desultory European interest had been shown in Africa to that point, amounting to little more than a patchwork of competing spheres of influence. These were mostly private concerns — chartered companies displaying a national flag — but here and there, territories were being annexed and occupied, and in general, a rather unhealthy mood of competition was incubating over the question of Africa.

Perhaps the best example of this was the Witwatersrand, the gold-bearing region of the Transvaal Republic, nominally a British sphere of influence and certainly the most important theatre of British capital adventure of the age. South Africa at that point was divided into four separate territories - two British colonies (Natal and Cape) and two independent Boer republics (Transvaal and Orange Free State) - and between these there existed enormous suspicion and antipathy. The superior weight of British capital and imperial reach allowed the British to dominate the Transvaal gold fields, but they did so very much to the chagrin of the Boer. The Boer were not by any means impoverished because of this, but as they prospered, they were ever vigilant toward any British threat against their sovereignty.

It was onto this rather tense economic and political stage that the Germans entered in 1884, annexing the territory of Damaraland, nominally the whole of modern-day Namibia, as a German colony. This immediately pitched the British into a fit of apprehension. What were German intentions? Was it the gold, the diamonds, the strategic ports, or all of the above? The British were acutely aware that the hatred felt toward them by the Boer could easily drive them into the arms of an opposing European power, and bearing in mind the ideological compatibility of Germany and Boer at that time, the Germans were in a position, should they choose, to wreak havoc on British interests in South Africa. As it turned out, Germany's acquisition of colonies in Africa would pave the way for some of the most important fighting of World War II generations later.

Meanwhile, for Germany's future, Bismarck thought it vital to form alliances that would isolate France. His continual efforts to unite Germany, Austria-Hungary, and Russia represented the most important foreign policy work in the waning years of his life. It was only after Bismarck's resignation and removal that the League of Three Emperors finally saw its end, allowing France and Russia to form an alliance that would prove crucial for World War I.

Wilhelm I, having worked with Bismarck for 27 years, died in 1888. His son, Frederick III, took the throne but followed his father in death only a few months later, which left the throne to Wilhelm's grandson, the 22-year-old Wilhelm II.[144]

---

[144] George O. Kent, 124-5.

Wilhelm II

Frederick III

Ironically, Wilhelm II's mother, Victoria, suspected many courtiers, especially Bismarck, of conspiring against her and Frederick III and depriving them of power by treating Wilhelm II as the true emperor. In turn, the dislike Wilhelm II had for his mother was only intensified by his father's short reign, and by the time Frederick III passed away, the rift between mother and son was so deep that it could hardly be mended. Bismarck watched with delight as the relationship between mother and son deteriorated, for he knew that he needed to begin to influence the future ruler long before the young Wilhelm II took over the throne. Bismarck, however, would learn that Wilhelm II had an independent streak.

Indeed, Bismarck and Wilhelm II were a mismatch from the beginning. Bismarck had previously been able to control the previous emperor through a mixture of genuine and protested loyalties and regular threats of resignation, but that would not be the case with Wilhelm II. The first great break between Wilhelm II and Bismarck came before the former even took power, after Wilhelm II expressed a desire for a war against Russia; Wilhelm held increasingly hostile views toward Russia ever since his second visit there in 1886, and anti-German feeling was prevalent in Russia because of Bismarck's support of Austria to the Russians' disadvantage in the Balkans. However, Bismarck was not willing to share Wilhelm's lust for war, because he was familiar with the complexities of internal Russian politics and did not see war as an inevitable result. Wilhelm shot back by publicly repudiating Bismarck's policy toward Russia and Austria, and though Bismarck retorted privately to a friend that he had no intention of going to war with Russia, in public he claimed that a war with Russia was a possibility. All the while, the two began drifting apart.

Wilhelm II's first act as the new emperor was to address the Prussian army, a fittingly symbolic choice since it set the tone of his whole reign and made clear military affairs would be the supreme expression of his interests. And as he had demonstrated earlier, he continued to battle vice. One of the first acts of the new sovereign was to wage a campaign against the drinking clubs popular among the officer corps; only a few weeks after assuming the throne, Wilhelm II ordered army commanders to prevent all army officers from frequenting such clubs.

The emperor then proceeded to tackle more serious matters. In the summer of 1888, acting on his belief that the officers' ranks were getting on in years, Wilhelm began to cull the ranks of the more elderly and feeble officers, leading to accusations that he was micromanaging who received key posts.[145] For example, Wilhelm appointed his long-time friend, General Count von Waldersee, as Chief of the General Staff, and the two began to make changes to numerous military positions. Part of what made General Count von Waldersee attractive to Wilhelm was his staunch anti-Russian attitude. In the same vein, Wilhelm insulated himself by his tendency to appoint likable officers as his adjutants, and in reference to these elegant soldiers who were chosen for their appearance and social standing, later Chancellor Prince Hohenlohe would call them the "Chinese wall." Wilhelm was also accused of taking revenge on officers who opposed him well before he ascended the throne.

Wilhelm's focus on military matters and his tendency to take advice and direction exclusively from a small coterie of military men had other effects as well. Even though he would end up ruling for 30 years, historians have pointed out that his connection with his subjects was weak and narcissistic. The sovereign was insulated from the realities of Imperial Germany by the fact that he had a very small group of close confidants, all of whom were dependent on the throne for their positions.

Nevertheless, Wilhelm sought to be the ruler of all his subjects despite that insulation, and in the early years of his reign, Wilhelm introduced reforms aimed at expanding his base of support. He made plans to open up the officer corps to the middle-classes, and he also appointed notable progressives to high profile posts in the military.[146] Through these measures, Wilhelm enjoyed considerable popularity with the working class, at least in the beginning. For a while, he was perceived as "the workers' King." It was due to the influence of Wilhelm's early tutor Hinzpeter that the young emperor paid such attention to the lower social classes. Wilhelm II believed that government must grant concessions to the poor as an antidote to Bismarck's repressive labor

[145] Cecil I, pg 125
[146] Cecil, 133

policies, and Wilhelm II was only in power for less than a year before his ideas were tested. Strikes began in the coal industry in the Rhineland and in Silesia in May 1889, leading Prussian troops to quell the violence. Wilhelm believed the strikes were caused by Polish Catholic fanatics, whom historians now say bore only part of the responsibility. Wilhelm's opinion was that the entire Rhineland had been neglected by the industrialists as soon as they made their quick profits. The Rhineland industrialists did not, in Wilhelm's opinion, create favorable conditions like those that existed in the state factories of Silesia, and Wilhelm was determined not to begin his reign with bloodshed. Thus, he ordered his military to protect workers against employers, which he believed was the only way to decrease the incidence of labor violence.

On the same front, the emperor allowed the first deputation of workers to visit the palace to express their grievances and expectations for an 8 hour work day. Wilhelm II urged the industrialists to negotiate with labor, which led to a settlement within two weeks, and he took great relish in the fact that he had been the cause of the agreement.[147] On the other hand, Bismarck was horrified; in his mind, the working class could never be appeased and had to be coerced into its proper position. Bismarck rejected the emperor's insistence that the working classes be brought on board the planning of social programs as equal participants. Although he had created social welfare legislation that was unique for Europe at the time, Bismarck believed the state should act repressively in the wake of socialist electoral victories. Bismarck was waging what he viewed as preventative class warfare.

The disagreement over how to deal with the strike in the Rhineland and Silesia was merely the first major argument between the two powerful personalities. The first conflict before an audience of public officials took place on May 12, 1889, at a meeting of ministers. Bismarck held that the situation should be allowed to worsen in order to allow a pretext for more sweeping action against the agitators, but the emperor expressed his viewpoint that the demands of the workers should be considered since any further worsening of the situation would weaken the Empire. As that debate made clear, it was apparent from the beginning that the chancellor would need to handle his boss carefully. The emperor obviously intended to be the dominant force in both domestic and foreign policy, and the chancellor quickly learned that he would have to adapt to the emperor's demands on every day matters.

However, after spending decades as the de facto dictator of the empire, Bismarck found it difficult to relinquish power. The year 1890 began with the two figures still arguing over policies toward workers, and the two squared off over the contents of Wilhelm's speech to open the parliament's annual meeting. The emperor insisted on appeasing the coalition of Social Democrats and their Catholic allies with a new round of socially progressive legislation that would protect the working class, while Bismarck's response was that he would rather resign than give in to the Social Democrats. The emperor opined to his confidants that the chancellor had become increasingly difficult to deal with, but he still needed Bismarck to help assure passage of

---

[147] Cecil, 135

an increasingly large military budget later in the spring.

On January 24, Wilhelm II opened the parliament with a detailed speech on the labor question; the miners' strikes of the previous year in the Rhineland had created an atmosphere that had to be dealt with. He admitted that the explosive growth of German industry had allowed exploitative publicly traded companies to come into existence, mistreating workers and pushing them into the willing arms of agitators. The success of socialist agitators was due, said the emperor, to government's inability to providing reforming labor legislation. The emperor struck a middle line by saying that the government must pass progressive legislation on the side of the working man without tolerating exorbitant demands that would injure Germany's ability to compete on the world market. In the same speech, he rejected the demands for an 8 hour work day and a 50% increase in wages that had been demanded by miners in the Rhineland.

As expected, Bismarck's response to the speech was negative, and by the end of January 1890, Wilhelm II had reached a decision on a replacement for Bismarck. He called General Leo von Caprivi, the commanding general of the Tenth Army Corps, to Berlin and told Caprivi that in the event of a final break with Bismarck, Caprivi would be his desired successor.

Caprivi

Meanwhile, by mid-February, Bismarck was hoping for an opportunity to use the ever growing possibility of a coup d'etat as a pretext for setting aside the constitution of 1871 and disbanding parliament. Recently held elections weakened Bismarck's position and required that in the future he make amends with the Catholic Center and Social Democrats, but the fear of a coup was not enough to put Bismarck and the Kaiser back on equal footing. As historian Michael Balfour put it in *The Kaiser and his Times*, when Bismarck was aware that time was running out on him, "All Bismarck's resources were deployed; he even asked Victoria to use her influence over her son on his behalf. But the wizard had lost his magic; his spells were powerless because they were exerted on people who did not respect them, and he who had so signally disregarded Kant's command to use people as ends in themselves had too small a stock of loyalty to draw on. As Lord Salisbury told Queen Victoria, "The very qualities which Bismarck fostered in the Emperor in order to strengthen himself when the Emperor Frederick should come to the throne have been the qualities by which he has been overthrown." The Empress, with what must have been a mixture of pity and triumph, told him that her influence with her son could not save him for he himself had destroyed it.

Despite the advice of advisers that he should sack the chancellor, Wilhelm II was still hesitant to do so. He was concerned about public opinion and the passage of the military budget, but due to an ongoing dispute over a document that the emperor requested from Bismarck, Bismarck submitted his resignation on March 19. He was finally finished with the chancellor.

A famous political cartoon, titled "Dropping the Pilot", depicts Bismarck leaving the ship of state while Wilhelm II looks on from the deck.

Though Wilhelm II publicly claimed Bismarck had retired due to ill health, Bismarck spent the rest of his life making it clear that he had served Wilhelm I faithfully and had no use for the new ruler. In his resignation, Bismarck made both his loyalties and disappointment clear: "Considering my attachment to service for the monarchy and for Your Majesty and the long-established relationship which I had believed would exist forever, it is very painful for me to terminate my accustomed relationship to the All Highest and to the political life of the Reich and Prussia...Judging from my impressions over the past weeks…I have reason to reverently assume that I am accommodating the wishes of Your Majesty with my request for discharge, and thus I am able to rely with certainty on the gracious approval of my request. I would have submitted the request for dismissal from my offices to Your Majesty earlier, had I not been under the impression that it was Your Majesty's wish to make use of the experience and talents of a loyal servant to His ancestors. Now that I am certain that Your Majesty does not require these, I may withdraw from political life without fearing that my decision will be condemned as untimely by public opinion."

Though Bismarck would continue to criticize the young emperor publicly, the two were reconciled at a meeting in 1894. By that time, Bismarck had lost his wife and his health. He died in July of 1898, having left instructions for his tombstone's inscription to be: "A Faithful German Servant of William I."[148]

For Bismarck, being a man and statesman were the same roles. Without political intrigue, Bismarck seemed to lack purpose, and he had been at the forefront of most major conflicts unfolding in the second half of the 19th century. Moreover, by leaving an indelible mark on Germany, Otto von Bismarck's presence would be felt in the coming conflicts headed Europe's way in the 20th century.

Online Resources

Other books about German history by Charles River Editors

Other books about Bismarck on Amazon

Further Reading

Barkin, Kenneth. "Otto Von Bismarck", The Latin Library. <latinlibrary.com> Accessed October 7, 2017.

--Bismarck on "Pragmatic" Colonization (June 26, 1884) Forging an Empire: Bismarckian Germany (1866 -1890) German History in Documents and Images.

--Bismarck, The Man and the Statesman; Being the Reflections and Reminiscences of Otto, Prince Von Bismarck. Vol 1. Ed., A.J. Butler. New York, London, Harper & Bros. 1898.

--Bismarck, The Man and the Statesman; Being the Reflections and Reminiscences of Otto, Prince Von Bismarck. Vol 2., Ed., A.J. Butler. New York, London, Harper & Bros. 1898.

Blumberg, Arnold ed., *Great Leaders, Great Tyrants?: Contemporary Views of World Rulers Who Made History.* Westport, CT: Greenwood Press, 1995. Craig, Gordon A. *Theodor Fontane: Literature and History in the Bismarck Reich.* New York: Oxford University Press, 1999.

---

[148] Ibid., 128-9.

Boissoneault, Lorraine. "Bismarck Tried to End Socialism's Grip—By Offering Government Healthcare." *Smithsonian Magazine*. July 14, 2017.

Cook, Michael. "How Bismarck Lost Kulturkampf.", *Crisis Magazine*, July 17, 2012.

Ebeling, Richard M. "Marching to Bismarck's Drummer: The Origins of the Modern Welfare State." *Foundation for Economic Education*. December 1, 2007.

--Ems Telegram, 1870. World War One Primary Documents. www.firstworldwar.com

Eyck, Erich. *Bismarck and the German Empire*. New York: W.W. Norton and Company, 1968.

Feuchtwanger, Edgar. "Bismarck, Prussia & German Nationalism," *History Review*, 2001.

Halsey, Francis W. and Bryan, William Jennings, eds., *The World's Famous Orations*, vol. 7 New York: Funk and Wagnalls, 1906.

Kent, George O. *Bismarck and His Times*. Carbondale, IL: Southern Illinois University Press, 1978.

Lay, Paul. "Interview: Jonathan Steinberg." *History Today*, Volume 2, Issue 9, September 2012.

Lerman, Katherine. *Bismarck: Profiles in Power*. London: Routledge; Taylor and Francis Group, 2004.

Lewis, Charlton T., ed., *The love letters of Bismarck; being letters to his fiancée and wife, 1846-1889; authorized by Prince Herbert von Bismarck and translated from the German under the supervision of Charlton T. Lewis*. New York: Harper, 1901.

Lougee, Robert W. "The Kulturkampf and Historical Positivism." Church History 23, no. 3 (1954): 219.

Otto von Bismarck, Reden 1847-1869 [Speeches, 1847-1869], ed., Wilhelm Schüßler, vol. 10, Bismarck: Collected Works], ed. Hermann von Petersdorff. Berlin: Otto Stolberg, 1924-35.

Pearce, Robert. "The Austro-Prussian War: Robert Pearce Examines the Factors That Led to Prussia's Victory in the German Civil War of 1866," *History Review*, no. 66 (2010).

Pflanze, Otto. *Bismarck and the Development of Germany: The Period of Unification, 1815-1871.* Princeton, NJ: Princeton University Press, 1971.

--P.G. Tait's poem on Bismark [sic.] ELIZABETH F LEWIS (NEE RUDGE) University of St

Andrews April 22, 2012.

--"Prussia and Austria: The Schleswig Holstein Question." *The New York Times*, June 11, 1865.

Steefel, Lawrence D. *Bismarck, the Hohenzollern Candidacy, and the Origins of the Franco-German War of 1870*. Cambridge, MA: Harvard University Press, 1962.

Steinberg, Jonathan. *Bismarck: A Life*. Oxford: Oxford University Press, 2011.

Taylor, A. J. P. *Bismarck: The Man and the Statesman*. New York: Knopf, 1955.

Wawro, Geoffrey. *The Austro-Prussian War: Austria's War with Prussia and Italy in 1866*. New York: Cambridge University Press, 1997.

Free Books by Charles River Editors

We have brand new titles available for free most days of the week. To see which of our titles are currently free, click on this link.

Discounted Books by Charles River Editors

We have titles at a discount price of just 99 cents everyday. To see which of our titles are currently 99 cents, click on this link.

Printed in Great Britain
by Amazon

63215720R00037